PUBLISHED BY:

FPMI Communications, Inc.
707 Fiber Street
Huntsville, AL 35801-5833

(205) 539-1850
Fax: (205) 539-0911

E-Mail: fpmi@aol.com
Internet: http://www.fpmi.com

ISBN 0-936295-65-1

By

RALPH R. SMITH

DENNIS K. REISCHL

AND

GARY A. KOCA

TABLE OF CONTENTS

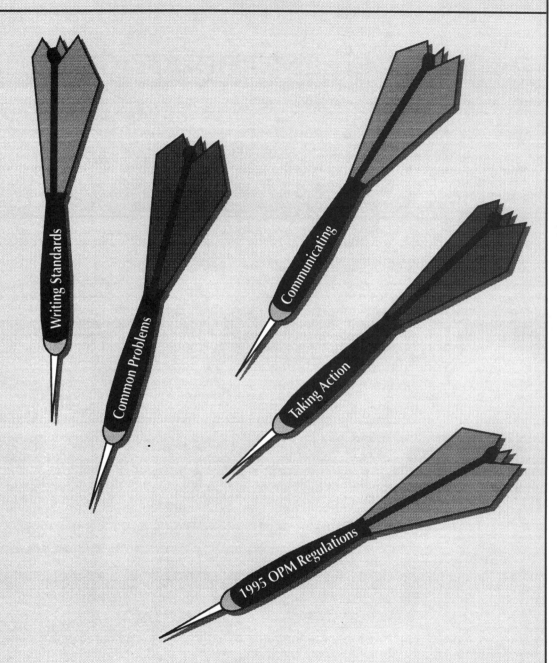

INTRODUCTION

There are a wide variety of systems and no two agency performance management systems are exactly alike. Even so, there have been a great many recent changes in performance management that affect all agencies. Developing, writing, and using effective performance standards is still at the heart of most performance management systems.

Performance management can be a difficult job. There are at least two reasons for this.

First, developing performance standards that outline how an employee is to perform a job is hard work. It requires you to:

> ✓ Think carefully about the duties and functions each employee performs;
>
> ✓ Break overall job duties down into separate, identifiable elements;
>
> ✓ Decide what constitutes fully successful performance; and, finally,
>
> ✓ Write in clear English how well an employee must perform the duties of a position to obtain a satisfactory performance rating.

Second, applying performance standards also requires substantial effort. To make them useful, you have to monitor the efforts of an employee, meet periodically to provide feedback, make necessary adjustments in performance plans, and develop ratings based on results rather than gut reactions.

PURPOSE

Keep the following in mind:

FIRST ————————————————————————————
Employees must know what is expected of them to perform successfully, and agency management expects you to write effective performance standards because it is one of your most important supervisory duties.

SECOND ————————————————————————————
Although writing effective performance standards is hard work, it is important to spend the time necessary to do it well. An organization that does not have well-written standards will not be able to use the performance appraisal system as an effective management tool or to deal with performance problems when they crop up.

This book will help you develop well-written, practical job elements and performance standards. Following the steps outlined in this book will improve your ability to write and implement performance standards. You will find the morale of your employees and efficiency of your organization improve as a result of a better managed organization in which all employees know their role and why they are important in accomplishing the agency's mission.

Why Are Performance Standards Important?

Why is it important to bother with performance standards? Most employees know what is expected of them and do reasonably well. And those who do not perform their work properly are usually easy to spot. So why spend time and effort trying to write down everything employees are supposed to do? Isn't that what a position description does anyway?

While these questions are understandable, they do not reflect the reality of life in the Federal service today. When the Civil Service Reform Act was enacted in 1978, it tied almost every important personnel management decision to employees' performance ratings. While recent changes in regulations from the Office of Personnel Management (OPM) have severed some decisions from the appraisal, it is still an important tool for managers.

For example, performance ratings influence:

➾ Who keeps or loses a job during a reduction-in-force (a RIF);

➾ Whether an employee should be retained in or removed from his position;

➾ Whether an employee gets a within-grade increase;

➾ Whether to select an employee for a job or to approve a career ladder promotion; or

➾ Whether an employee receives a performance award.

In short, performance ratings impact every employee. So it is important that ratings be fair and based on actual performance, rather than personality traits or popularity. And it is important to a manager who wants to have an efficient organization to have accurate, fair ratings as well.

In order to make certain employees are rated fairly, each supervisor must spell out what tasks she expects an employee to perform, and to specify how well the employee must perform these tasks in order to be rated at a satisfactory—or, as it is often called, "fully successful"—level.

Equipped with clear performance plans, supervisors and managers are in a better position to identify acceptable, superior and inadequate performance, and to take appropriate steps after the rating is given. In other words, when performance can be objectively observed and measured, managers

Equipped with clear performance plans, supervisors and managers are in a better position to identify acceptable, superior and inadequate performance, and to take appropriate steps.

and supervisors are better able to determine what corrective steps are necessary, and to justify performance awards. So, as you can see, the creation of clear, accurate performance standards is in your interest as well as that of the employees who work for you.

Although supervisors and managers often find it hard to make time to write solid performance standards, it is essential that you do so. Spending the time to develop effective standards now will save a lot more time later. Why? Because poorly written standards make it harder to deal with substandard performers, more difficult to reward good performers, and increase the number of personnel problems and grievances that eat up productive time. As the auto mechanic used to say in the commercial urging preventive maintenance and oil changes, "You can pay me now or pay me later." Inevitably, it is preferable to pay with less time up front preventing problems, rather than more time later trying to fix them.

Steps In The Performance Management Cycle

As a Federal supervisor, you are responsible for developing and carrying out a performance appraisal plan for each of your employees. These are the steps you will be taking to properly do this important job:

☞ Encourage your employees, including teams of employees, to help in developing performance standards and in the overall performance appraisal process.

☞ Identify major functions each employee performs, and break these into separate, important tasks, called *performance elements*.

☞ Determine which performance elements are critically important to successfully meeting the requirements of each employee's position.

☞ Identify how well each performance element must be performed to merit a rating of satisfactory/fully successful.

☞ Develop performance standards spelling out performance expectations for each performance element.

☞ Communicate performance *standards* and performance *elements* clearly to each employee.

☞ Monitor each employee's performance to ensure compliance with performance requirements.

☞ Provide assistance necessary to help employees meet performance expectations set out in their performance standards.

☞ Evaluate each employee by comparing performance on each performance element to the performance standards you have established.

☞ Take appropriate action based on performance, such as performance awards, or corrective steps to improve substandard performance.

Each of these items will be addressed separately. By following them, you should be able to properly implement a performance appraisal plan that will satisfy legal requirements, assist employees in improving their performance, and justify personnel management decisions based on objective performance ratings.

A CAUTIONARY NOTE: DEALING WITH EMPLOYEES REPRESENTED BY A UNION

Before we further explore developing and implementing performance standards, you need to be aware of special requirements that may be involved in dealing with employees represented by a labor union. If any of the employees under your supervision are covered by a labor agreement, there may be additional requirements you must meet. In fact, your organization's partnership committee may provide guidance as agencies move to implement the flexibility permitted under OPM's regulations.

Because these requirements may vary among agencies, you should thoroughly review any labor agreement applicable to your employees early in the performance appraisal process.

If you are not sure if any of your employees are covered by a union contract, contact your agency's personnel or labor relations specialists for assistance. These specialists will be able to advise you of any special requirements of the labor contract.

DEFINITIONS

Here are several commonly used terms that describe the Federal performance appraisal system. Because these terms will be used throughout this book, you should know what they mean.

APPRAISAL
The process used to evaluate an employee. This is often called a *performance rating*. It is an assessment of an employee's past performance based on a comparison of the employee's work with standards established in the performance appraisal plan.

APPRAISAL PERIOD
The period established by a performance appraisal system during which an employee's performance is observed in order to formally evaluate it at the end of the period. Most agencies use an appraisal period of one year, but require a shorter period on which to base an appraisal.

APPRAISAL PROGRAM
The specific procedures and requirements established under the policies and parameters of an agency appraisal system. One agency's system may contain several programs.

APPRAISAL SYSTEM
A performance appraisal system that has been established by an agency in accordance with law (Subchapter 1, chapter 43, of Title 5, United States Code) and OPM regulations.

CRITICAL ELEMENT
A performance element so important that unacceptable performance by an employee on one critical element would result in an overall unacceptable performance rating and corrective action, such as a reassignment, downgrade or removal from Federal service.

NON-CRITICAL ELEMENT
An important dimension of individual, team or organizational performance that may be used in assigning a summary rating.

PERFORMANCE

The accomplishment of assigned tasks or responsibilities in comparison with the specific performance standards established in the employee's performance appraisal plan.

PERFORMANCE ELEMENT

A distinguishable task or unit of work required by an employee's position. Performance elements state the individual major responsibilities assigned to an employee.

PERFORMANCE MANAGEMENT

This is the total process of observing an employee's performance over a period of time; comparing the performance to the performance requirements contained in the performance appraisal plan; and then evaluating the performance by giving the employee a performance rating. Performance management includes working with employees on a daily basis to improve their performance.

PERFORMANCE PLAN

A collection of critical and non-critical elements and their performance standards.

PERFORMANCE STANDARD

A statement that outlines specific tasks and duties that an employee is expected to perform and how well these must be accomplished in order to justify a particular rating level, such as "fully successful" or "outstanding." It can include items such as quality, quantity, timeliness, and manner of performance.

PROGRESS REVIEW

A review of an employee's progress in meeting established performance standards at various points during the performance period.

Chapter One

Writing Performance Elements & Standards

IDENTIFYING PERFORMANCE ELEMENTS

The performance elements of a position are basic to a performance appraisal plan. Everything else in the plan flows from the performance elements. Therefore, it is necessary to understand and correctly apply this concept in order to develop a solid performance plan. A performance element is:

A distinguishable task or unit of work required by an employee's position. Performance elements state the individual major responsibilities assigned to an employee.

A performance element can be — but does not have to be — derived from a position description. A set of individual or organizational goals can be another starting point for developing performance elements.

There are two questions that you should consider when reviewing an employee's duties to identify performance elements. These are:

1. Is an individual task an important part of an employee's overall job?

For example, a supervisory nurse may perform many tasks as part of her job, including preparing and administering medications to patients and approving requests for sick and annual leave.

But preparing medications is an important, central task of the job, while approving leave requests is only an incidental duty. Accordingly, preparing medications should be considered as a performance element, but approving leave probably should not, or may be part of a larger element such as "human resources management responsibilities."

2. Is the individual task part of an overall function or duty?

For example, laying bricks is an individual task that a mason would likely perform, but he probably is involved in constructing walls of concrete block and natural stone as well. In this case, it would not make sense to write individual elements for each type of material. Rather, the mason's bricklaying should be part of an element that outlines his responsibility for constructing walls of various masonry materials.

Remember, your objective in identifying performance elements is to pinpoint the major, important tasks and duties that the employee performs so you can establish performance expectations. You want to avoid getting bogged down in minor details of the position. You also want to avoid breaking every duty into small fragments and winding up with an overly-long list of very narrow performance elements. For example, consider a human resource management element instead of a series of smaller elements for supervisors.

Which Performance Elements Should You Include?

With these objectives in mind, how can you determine which performance elements should be included in a performance plan? Carefully answering these questions about each task will help you identify performance elements:

How often is the task performed?
If a task is not performed frequently it is less likely to be a strong candidate for becoming a performance element. On the other hand, if it is a routine, important duty, it should be seriously considered.

How much time does the employee spend doing the task?
If a task comes up frequently but requires very little time when the employee is working on it, ask yourself whether the task is important enough to be rated.

Is the task in the employee's position description?
An employee's position description generally outlines the most important aspects of the job. If a task is not reflected here, it may not be a good candidate to be identified as a performance element. If a task is not in the position description but you still think it is important enough to be a performance element, you may wish to include it anyway (and possibly update the position description).

Does the employee have control over the function or task?
If the outcome of a task is beyond the employee's control, it is not fair to hold the employee accountable and it should not be included as a performance element. For example: If you are providing information to individuals, and there's no way to determine how many clients you serve each week, it is better to hold employees accountable for the quality and timeliness of service rather than the number of customers served.

Do similar positions have the same duty assignments? If other employees are doing essentially the same job, you should determine whether a particular task has been included as a performance element in their performance standards. Because the primary goal of the performance appraisal system is to measure performance fairly and objectively, people in similar positions should have the same or similar performance elements. Differences in performance plans should be based on identifiable differences in work.

Was the task considered in classifying the position?
The job classification process takes certain tasks into account in determining the proper grade of a job. Normally, these are the most important parts of a position and should be listed as performance elements of a performance plan. Again, these tasks should also be reflected in the position description.

How difficult is the task?
The most difficult tasks are normally the ones you will be most likely to include as performance elements. Often difficult tasks will also turn up under the other considerations listed above, such as the amount of time spent by the employee on a task.

What are potential adverse consequences if there is an error in performing the task?
Those tasks and duties that have the largest potential adverse impact on other employees or the organization will normally be identified as performance elements.

What impact does the task have on the organization's mission?
You should consider a task that will impact an organization's ability to accomplish its mission or meet its goals as a better candidate to be listed in the performance plan as a performance element than a task that is not closely related to the goals of the organization.

When applied with common sense, these identifying factors should help you determine what performance elements you should put into an employee's performance plan. While there are no set rules on the number of performance elements required, most plans will contain at least three performance elements, but usually no more than eight.

WRITING PERFORMANCE ELEMENTS

Once you have identified the major tasks and duties that are performance elements for a position, you are ready to start the next step: Putting the performance elements in simple written form. Although there are several ways to do this, the following examples outline a straightforward, popular way of writing performance elements. Avoid just copying the language of the position description into performance elements, since that format is usually not useful in appraising performance.

A well-written performance element is simple and easy to understand. It should consist of an action verb and an object. For example:

Action Verb	Object
Types	letters and memoranda
Prepares	weekly reports
Trains	subordinates
Audits	travel vouchers

As you can see, performance elements boil down the main tasks of a position into very simple statements.

Once you have done this, then you should add language that will briefly explain the purpose of the particular job element. For example:

> ✖ Types letters and memoranda *in order to* communicate with the clients of the organization.
>
> ✖ Submits weekly reports *in order to* track the case load in the office.
>
> ✖ Trains subordinates *in order to* increase productivity.
>
> ✖ Audits travel vouchers *in order to* track travel expenses.

Using this format is not something you have to do. But if you use an action verb and an object this way, it will be easier for you to write performance standards that will be easy to understand and to explain to employees.

Once the performance elements have been established and written, your next step is to decide which performance elements you think should be identified as *critical elements*.

WORKSHOP

Using the position description and your knowledge of the job, develop a set of performance elements for a position you supervise.

Write these elements down in the method suggested on pages 22-23 (Action verb/noun/additional language).

1. _____
   _____
   _____
   _____

2. _____
   _____
   _____
   _____

3. _____
   _____
   _____
   _____

4. _____
   _____
   _____
   _____

5. _____

_____

_____

_____

6. _____

_____

_____

_____

7. _____

_____

_____

_____

8. _____

_____

_____

_____

STOP!

If you have more than eight performance elements, consider combining some until you have eight or fewer elements.

IDENTIFYING CRITICAL ELEMENTS

Once you have developed a list of performance elements you want to include in an employee's performance plan, you must designate at least one — and probably more — of these elements as *critical elements*. Remember, a critical element is:

A performance element so important that unacceptable performance by an employee on one critical element would result in an overall unacceptable performance rating and corrective action, such as a reassignment, downgrade or removal from Federal service.

There is no limit on the number of critical elements that may be included in a performance plan.

•

But there must be at least one in every employee's performance plan.

There is no limit on the number of critical elements that may be included in a performance plan. But there must be at least one in every employee's performance plan. Most plans contain from three to six critical elements. Some plans may also list performance elements that are not identified as critical, but are included as elements because the supervisor considers them too important to leave out.

What Makes An Element Critical?

How do you select critical elements from among the performance elements you have written? These considerations should help you.

- *Focus on those performance elements that are important in accomplishing the mission of your organization.* For example, properly connecting electrical wires and inspecting electrical equipment are very important to an electrician's job and, because of this, they are good candidates for becoming the critical elements of a performance plan.

Focus on elements that are important in accomplishing the mission of your organization.

•

Select elements that are at the core of an employee's position.

•

Zero in on elements that must be performed well to avoid serious consequences.

the shop area is unlikely to justify a reduction in grade or removal from Federal service, you will probably decide not to designate this performance element as critical.

- *Select those elements at the core of an employee's position.* For example, the heart of a safety engineer's job might involve careful inspection of equipment to determine compliance with safety codes. If so, it should be included as a critical element.

- *Zero in on elements that must be performed well to avoid serious adverse consequences.* For example, if legal briefs must be filed within specified deadlines to avoid dismissal or loss of important cases, timely filing should be included among the critical elements.

On the other hand, cleaning up the immediate shop area may also be in an electrician's job description but is not of considerable importance to performing an electrician's duties. Since failing to properly clean up

WORKSHOP

Go back to your list of performance elements on pages 24 & 25. Designate with an asterisk those elements you consider to be critical. In other words:

- Important in accomplishing your mission
- At the core of an employee's position
- Must be performed to avoid adverse consequences

NOTE:

If your agency moves to a system which eliminates non-critical elements, you will only need to concern yourself with critical elements.

Developing Performance Standards

Once you have written the performance elements and identified the critical elements of a job, your next step will be to develop performance standards. Before you can develop an effective performance standard, it will help you to know what it is! One common definition of a performance standard is:

A clear statement that outlines specific tasks and duties that an employee is expected to perform as well as how well these must be accomplished to justify a particular rating level, such as "fully successful" or "outstanding."

A performance standard clearly states the specific tasks and duties an employee is expected to perform and how well these must be accomplished to justify a particular rating level.

The stated level of achievement that identifies how well a task must be performed may be based on the quality, quantity, or timeliness of work, or upon a specified manner of carrying out particular duties or tasks.

In short, a performance standard consists of two items: First, a clear statement of the specific duties that the employee is expected to perform. Second, an equally clear statement of how well the employee is expected to obtain the described results, or the manner in which certain duties must be performed.

YOUR OBJECTIVE

Your objective in writing a performance standard is to spell out for the employee exactly what she is expected to do to earn a particular rating. To decide whether the standard you have set meets the definition given above, there are several key questions you should ask.

> *Your objective in writing a performance standard is to spell out to the employee exactly what she is expected to do to earn a particular rating.*

The next several sections of this book will explain why you want to ask these questions, and how to develop answers that will help you in writing effective performance standards.

KEY QUESTIONS

❑ Does the standard address the accomplishment of a particular performance element rather than focus on a conduct requirement, such as coming to work on time?

❑ Does the standard address the quantity, quality, timeliness or manner of performing an important task or duty?

❑ Does the standard clearly explain how well a task must be performed in order to merit a particular rating?

❑ Does the standard require performance that is observable and measurable?

❑ Does the standard set different levels of performance for different ratings in performing a particular performance element?

❑ Does the standard require reasonable but not perfect performance in order to qualify for a "fully successful" rating?

❑ Is the standard clear enough to be fully and completely understandable to the employee who works under it?

QUANTITY, QUALITY AND TIMELINESS

The Civil Service Reform Act and implementing regulations require supervisors to develop performance standards that evaluate an employee's performance on the basis of objective criteria. This means that "subjective" feelings, reactions and perceptions should be avoided by focusing on matters that can be observed, measured and verified. While standards do not need to be quantitative, they should be measurable and observable. One of the best ways to do this is to establish criteria that clearly state the required quantity, quality, and timeliness of job performance.

QUANTITY

Quantity refers to the amount of work produced within a specific time. Generally it is stated in terms of a number of items an employee must produce or complete within a day, week, month or more.

For example, using the performance element *Audits travel vouchers in order to track travel expenses*, a performance standard reflecting quantity might require that the employee: "Completely audits an average of twenty-five travel vouchers per week."

QUALITY

Quality refers to how well a task is performed or how good, accurate or error-free the final product is expected to be. For example, using the job element *Trains subordinates in order to increase productivity*, a quality-oriented performance standard might require that: "On a grading scale of 1-5, the course evaluations submitted by participants must reflect an average overall course rating of 2.5 or more." If your position lends itself to error rates, numerical standards are probably appropriate. If not, a narrative, non-quantitative approach might be better. For example, *Written reports meet agency and customer needs* will allow you to focus on the overall product instead of merely counting errors.

TIMELINESS

Timeliness means when or how quickly a task must be completed by the employee. That is, the extent to which work must be accomplished within specified time frames. For example, using the job element *Submits weekly reports in order to track the case load in the office*, a timeliness-oriented performance standard might be: "Quarterly reports must be received in final format with certifying signature no later than 5 calendar days after the end of the quarter." A less quantitative standard may express it as *Quarterly reports must meet agency deadlines*.

Keep in mind that these are only examples demonstrating what is meant by quantity, quality, and timeliness. As the supervisor, only you can decide whether these examples are appropriate for use in a specific performance plan.

These three items — quantity, quality, and timeliness — may be used separately or in combination to develop standards. However, it is not necessary that each standard you write must contain all three. Use your own judgment and knowledge of the job to decide which of these are best in a particular performance plan. After all, only you are sufficiently familiar with the work in your organization to determine what is and is not appropriate in a performance standard.

Is The Standard Measurable?

As noted previously, an important factor in making performance standards objective is constructing them so that employees' actual performance is observable and measurable. In order to be measurable, a standard must make it possible to determine and demonstrate how well the employee carried out the required tasks.

Measurability is not necessarily synonymous with quantitative. However, in considering the measurability of a proposed standard, ask yourself whether you would be able to show another person objective proof substantiating the employee's level of performance. Remember, if a standard is not measurable, it is not valid.

Here are some examples of measurable standards:
✔ Audits a minimum of 25 vouchers per week.
✔ Drafts official agency responses to Congressional inquiries within 3 days of receipt.

> *A standard must make it possible to determine and demonstrate how well the employee carried out the required tasks.*

✔ Letters and memoranda are typed with sufficient accuracy to contain no more than 3 typographical errors in any random sample of 100 document pages.

How would you like to explain your rating of employees under these standards which are really task statements?
✔ Provides a full and accurate response to cases.
✔ Processes staffing request forms in a prompt and courteous manner.
✔ Routinely provides guidance and advice that falls within the bounds of agency policy in response to telephone inquiries.

See the difference? The key question, obviously, is "How would I be able to explain to someone outside the organization that the employee did or did not work up to expectations?" If you cannot see how you would be able to do that, chances are the standard you have written is not measurable or does not lend itself to being measured quantitatively.

WHAT ABOUT PROFESSIONAL EMPLOYEES?

A complaint sometimes voiced by supervisors is that the performance appraisal system will not work for professional employees because their work is simply not measurable. The nature of their work and the complexity of these positions often make the task of developing performance standards for professional positions more challenging.

> *The nature of a professional's work and the complexity of these positions make the task of developing performance standards more challenging.*

Nevertheless, performance standards can and must be developed for professional positions. Some aspects of professionals' jobs probably lend themselves to the traditional measurements of quantity, quality and timeliness. In other parts of their work, however, that approach may not be practical. In those areas, you may want to consider using so-called *manner of performance* standards.

Manner Of Performance Standards

A *manner of performance* standard differs from more traditional standards in that it describes in detail how an employee is expected to go about performing a particular function or task. Traditional standards focus upon the expected outcome in terms of quantity, quality, or timeliness. Manner of performance standards focus more on how the work is accomplished on the theory that correct procedures will lead to satisfactory outcomes.

This type of standard is also less objective. Nevertheless, some agencies have found this approach helpful in writing standards for work that does not easily lend itself to measurements of quantity, quality or timeliness.

Here is an example of a manner of performance standard:

> Written reports are well-written and understandable to the client. (Assumes that positive or negative comments are received, or that the supervisor asks the client if he could understand the report.)

Note that this standard does not focus on how many reports are completed, how many errors are allowable, or how fast the work must be done. Instead, it concentrates on a more general assessment of the work.

Even manner of performance standards must ultimately provide some way of measuring success. The previous standard —"Written reports are well-written and understandable to the client"— must somehow be measured in practice. Either you would have to add a *specific* measure to the standard — "On no more than three occasions were reports not well written or understandable" — or leave it as is and, instead, provide examples of written reports that are not well-written or understandable.

And where can you get this information? Your own assessment of the quality of the report, and you may want to consider the reaction from the client (or customer). What better way to assure you are paying attention to your customers than asking them what they think of the quality? (Keep in mind that a "customer" does not have to be someone outside your agency. In many cases, it is another office within your organization that is your customer.)

Will this approach stand the scrutiny of outside review when the inevitable appeal comes? Well, nothing's a guarantee, but the Merit Systems Protection Board (MSPB) has held it's not necessary to have quantitative standards as long as supervisors:

> *What better way to assure you are paying attention to your customers than asking them what they think of the quality?*

 a) assure that employees understand the standards (What do I mean by a well-written report?),

b) provide clear feedback to employees when they are not meeting the standards (specific examples),

c) provide a true opportunity period to improve, and

d) take actions only after the first three steps have been taken.

So what happens if your standards don't meet these tests? Any action you take based on poor performance or perhaps the rating itself may be overturned when an employee files a grievance or an appeal.

What About Standards For Different Rating Levels?

Some agency performance systems require that supervisors develop more than one level of performance standards for each performance element. In other words, when you write a performance standard for a rating of *fully successful*, some agency performance appraisal systems require that you also develop a standard for a rating above and below the fully successful level.

If your agency's plan requires this, the same guidelines still apply. The difference is that you must develop and write more than one level of achievement for the employee.

There are two primary ways to do this. One is by requiring somewhat better or lower performance on the same tasks identified in the fully successful standard. For example, if the fully successful standard requires the audit of at least 25 vouchers per week, the *minimally satisfactory* might require only 15, and the *outstanding* more than 35.

A second, and often better way of drawing a difference between the rating levels is by including or dropping various tasks from a performance element. For example, at the fully successful level you might require that a clerk identify and correct typographical and grammatical errors in reviewing correspondence. At the *outstanding* level you might also require that the clerk be able to identify awkward or improper phrasing and suggest specific improvements. And at the *minimally satisfactory* level you might be willing to settle for identifying and correcting typographical errors.

Finally, there is nothing that prevents you from mixing both approaches in developing a particular performance standard.

In order to decide how many levels of achievement must be included in the performance plan for employees under your supervision, check with the personnel office servicing your organization.

WORKSHOP

Based on the guidance we've just provided, try writing some performance standards for one or two of the elements you identified on pages 24 and 25.

1. _____
_____
_____
_____
_____
_____
_____
_____
_____
_____

2. _____
_____
_____
_____
_____
_____
_____
_____
_____
_____
_____
_____

Common Problems

COMMON PROBLEMS

Now that you have gotten this far into the performance management process, it will help you to closely review the standards you have written. There are several common errors that crop up in writing standards.

Fortunately, while these errors are quite common, most of them are easy to avoid if you know what you are looking for and understand why they create problems.

The extra time you take to correct problems now can save you a great deal of time — and problems — later on.

If you don't avoid these problems, they can come back to haunt you later on — especially if you become involved in trying to take corrective action based on an employee's poor performance. The extra time you take to correct problems now can save you a great deal of time — and problems — later on.

IS IT PERFORMANCE OR CONDUCT?

When you write a performance standard, you should address what you expect from an employee in performing the job. Avoid using conduct-related issues as a performance standard. For example, if you have an

Avoid using conduct-related issues as a performance standard.

employee whom you believe is abusing sick leave, it may be tempting to write a standard like this: "The incumbent will not use more than 5 days of sick leave during the year."

But this is not a good standard because it concerns a conduct issue: The inappropriate use of sick leave. It does not directly address how well the employee has performed assigned tasks.

A better approach is to write the performance standard along the lines of "The incumbent must initiate and complete five or more projects during the rating period." Then, if the projects are not completed, address this problem rather than the sick leave usage used in the first example. The first standard attempts to deal with misconduct, the second focuses on performance.

★ Performance standards address how well an employee performs a particular job task or duty, such as typing letters, completing engineering drawings, processing claim forms, and the like.

★ Conduct issues involve whether an employee has complied with a particular rule or agency code of conduct. For example, whether the employee has come to work on time, whether she has followed safety requirements, or whether she has carried out a direct order.

★ Poor performance usually involves a situation in which an employee intends or tries to accomplish job requirements, but is unable to do so for any of a variety of reasons.

★ Misconduct usually involves situations in which an employee deliberately breaks a rule, or fails to complete a work assignment intentionally.

As a general rule, in those areas in which you expect and require 100% perfect compliance — such as always coming to work on time, or always wearing safety glasses in the shop — it is better to leave such matters out of performance standards. Deal with failures to meet such requirements as rule infractions instead and correct them, when necessary, through discipline, not performance ratings.

It May Be Objective, But Is It Practical?

Avoid falling into the trap of developing a performance standard that is objective but not practical to measure. For example, one of the job elements listed above was "Audits travel vouchers in order to track travel expenses." One objective standard would be "25 travel vouchers will be audited each day and no more than 3 of these travel vouchers will be returned because of errors."

At first glance, this looks like an excellent performance standard. It is objective and also allows flexibility in granting a higher rating than fully successful. But keep in mind that this standard will require you to know how many travel vouchers are actually audited each day, and how many of these were returned

> *Avoid developing a performance standard that is objective but not practical to measure.*

with errors. If this standard is used but the essential information is not usually available, the standard is useless.

A similar problem arises when standards specify performance based on percentages of errors. Do not use them unless it will be practical for you to actually compute the percentage figures reflected in the standard without a great deal of investigation and number crunching.

Remember to write performance standards based on information that will be available to you when rating the employee. If the information will not be readily available to use in applying a proposed standard, or is not worth trying to get, develop a different one.

Is It A Backwards Standard?

A *backwards* standard is one that describes unacceptable or unsatisfactory performance rather than explaining what the employee is supposed to do to perform at an acceptable level.

For example, one supervisor wrote a standard like this to describe performance that was minimally successful: "No agenda for annual Energy Awareness Week is developed. No more than six conservation articles for the base newspaper are written."

In other words, the standard tells us what the employee will not or

> *Ask yourself whether a proposed performance standard explains to you what the employee is supposed to accomplish.*

should not do. The standard literally says that if the employee *does not* write six articles, he meets the specified standard for marginal performance. Accordingly, it qualifies as a backwards standard.

To avoid backward standards, ask yourself whether a proposed performance standard explains to you what it is the employee is supposed to accomplish. If it only tells you what he will not accomplish, it needs rewriting.

Is The Standard Absolute?

An absolute standard is one that does not allow any genuine margin for error. Under an absolute standard, an employee who fails once or in a very low percentage of cases to perform perfectly will automatically receive an unacceptable or unsatisfactory rating on that element.

For example, in a case in which an employee was required to make no more than three data entry errors per month, the Merit Systems Protection Board found that the standard called for an accuracy rate of over 99% to obtain a fully successful rating. It found the standard to be absolute and inappropriate in overturning the agency's performance-based adverse action against the employee.

> *Under an absolute standard, an employee who fails once or in a low percentage of cases will automatically receive an unacceptable or unsatisfactory rating on that element.*

While an absolute standard does not violate the law, it is usually considered by courts and the Merit Systems Protection Board to be an abuse of an agency's discretion to establish standards in all but a very few situations.

Although it is relatively rare, there are some jobs in which an absolute standard is necessary. If a single failure to perform at an acceptable level could result in death, injury, breach of security or significant loss of money, an absolute standard may be appropriate. You don't want an air traffic controller to be 99% accurate, when you are a passenger in an airplane!

For example, consider the following standard one supervisor wrote for a receptionist:

"There will be no substantiated instances on the part of the incumbent of rudeness, curtness, or use of abusive language to any visitor, staff member or telephone caller. One proven case of such behavior will justify an unsatisfactory rating on this element."

● *Does this element establish an absolute standard?*

Yes, since it requires absolute perfection to obtain a satisfactory rating on this element.

● *Is this element likely to pass muster as involving potential injury, death, great monetary loss, or violation of national security?*

Obviously not. Although courtesy is undoubtedly an important part of a receptionists' job, his failure to properly greet a single visitor will not have sufficiently devastating consequences to justify an absolute standard. Accordingly, this standard would not hold up under review by the MSPB or a court.

● Bonus Question: *How could this supervisor deal with a situation in which this receptionist occasionally makes clearly rude and inappropriate remarks to visitors?*

By warning the employee that such behavior is contrary to her direct instructions, and will result in disciplinary action. In other words, if perfection is required but the issue will not justify an absolute standard, it is usually better to deal with the matter as a *conduct* matter.

QUANTITATIVE OR NON-QUANTITATIVE STANDARDS?

As Hamlet said, "That is the question." And one that has confounded supervisors, managers, employees and personnel offices since the passage of the Civil Service Reform Act.

The dilemma is that it's pretty easy for someone working at McDonald's to be under a set of quantitative performance standards. How many orders the employee took per hour, how many mistakes he made, and how many customers had valid complaints about the employee's service.

Many Federal agencies are in a service business, and it's hard to quantify the service that employees provide. While it may be possible to quantify performance standards for employees who provide a tangible product, can you really quantify the service provided by your human resources management office or a NASA scientist?

On the other hand, it's clear that quantitative standards, **when**

> *Quantitative standards, when appropriate, are the easiest standards to deal with.*

appropriate, are the easiest standards to deal with. They are easy to understand, can be easily communicated to employees, and can be assessed because the measurement is right there in the standard. Manner of performance standards are much more difficult to assess through the use of numbers and percentages.

So what can we finally say about performance standards using numbers and percentages? If the positions you supervise lend themselves to a quantitative approach, by all means use that approach. If, on the other hand, you've been trying to measure performance without any success, why not try manner of performance standards?

It beats trying to determine how many patients your nurses aides can place in life threatening situations per year before you call them less than fully successful!

DON'T WORRY,
BE CONFIDENT

Don't let these few examples of common mistakes mislead you into thinking that you cannot write effective performance standards. You can, simply by following in an organized manner the steps we have outlined so far. Remember, there is no single best method for writing performance standards for every position.

Some positions allow straightforward objective measurement, while others may require more descriptive approaches with less precise measurement. If you take the time to review the steps outlined above and use them in writing your performance standards, you will be able to handle the task.

Do not be discouraged if your first attempt at writing standards does not result in a masterpiece. Writing good performance standards is not easy; like most other skills, it requires practice and attention to fully master the process. On the other hand, remember that there

> *Writing good performance standards requires practice and attention.*

are very few limits on you in developing performance standards. With careful thought and reasonable effort, you will be able to develop measurable standards that will serve the dual purpose of clearly telling employees what is expected of them and allowing you to maximize the productivity of your human resources.

Finally, remember you are not alone. Don't hesitate to call on your servicing personnel office for assistance. Your agency employs people who are specialists in the area of writing performance standards and they will be able to help you in developing and writing effective performance standards. They are a resource available for your use, so don't feel shy about asking for help.

WORKSHOP

Take the standards you developed on page 39. Rework them by taking a look at the following areas:

- Conduct or performance
- Objective but not practical
- Backwards standards
- Absolute standards
- Quantitative or Non-Quantitative

1. _____
_____
_____
_____
_____
_____
_____
_____
_____

2. _____
_____
_____
_____
_____
_____
_____
_____
_____

COMMUNICATING PERFORMANCE STANDARDS TO EMPLOYEES

Once you have written performance elements and standards, your next task is to communicate them to the employees for whom you developed them. As you know, it will take time and thought to develop and write elements and standards. But if they are not clearly understood by the affected employees, they remain nothing more than words on a piece of paper — a waste of time for everyone involved. There are several steps you can take that will help you successfully accomplish this aspect of the performance appraisal process.

> *Make sure you understand the overall performance plan; what elements and standards are included; and why you have included them in the plan.*

STEP ONE
PREPARE FOR THE MEETING

The first step is to prepare for the meeting. Make sure you understand the overall performance plan; what elements and standards are included in the employee's plan; and why you have included them in the plan. A lack of understanding will convey the impression that the work you have done and the work you expect the employee to do is indefinite or not important. Most employees will sense your attitude and react accordingly.

Remember that this meeting is to convey your expectations for her performance throughout the next year. The actions you take in this meeting or the attitudes you convey may make the difference between exceptional and mediocre or even substandard performance.

STEP TWO
ENSURE PRIVACY

The second step to ensuring successful communication of the performance appraisal plan is to hold a meeting in a setting conducive to a private discussion. Conducting a meeting to convey performance expectations in a public area will not encourage a frank and open discussion of the plan you have developed, and it may put the employee on the defensive. Arrange the setting as you would for any discussion that is important and for which privacy is essential.

STEP THREE
UNDERSTAND YOUR PURPOSE

Have the purpose of the meeting set firmly in your own mind. The purpose should be twofold:

- First, to convey your expectations regarding his on-the-job performance to the employee.

- Second, to encourage the employee to react to these standards and elements.

Meeting this second objective will require you to carefully listen to the employee's reaction and to any suggestions the employee may have for improving or adjusting. Although the final call is yours, approaching such meetings with an open mind can result in your finding genuine improvements to your original performance plan.

Remember that while you have the authority to establish the final content of the plan, if the employee does not accept or understand it, the plan will not be as useful a tool as it should be.

STEP FOUR
EXPLAIN THE PURPOSE

> *Each employee should leave the meeting knowing the expectations that have been established for individual performance.*

Explain to the employee the nature and purpose of the performance appraisal system. Each employee should leave the meeting knowing the expectations that have been established for her individual performance throughout the next performance appraisal cycle. She should also understand that the rating given will be used as a basis for making important personnel decisions, such as awards and promotions. You will find that many employees do not fully understand how the performance system works or how ratings are used. As a result, they may be fearful or suspicious of it. If you can help clear up their fears and suspicions by giving them a clear, simple explanation of how the overall system works, they are likely to be more efficient and productive.

STEP FIVE
EXPLAIN THE ELEMENTS AND STANDARDS

> *Remember that if the plan is a joint effort between you and the employee, it will be more acceptable... and more successful.*

Explain each performance element and performance standard. Encourage him to ask questions and to provide input into the plan. Remember that if the plan is one that is a joint effort between you and the employee, it will be more acceptable (and hence more successful) than one that is just handed to the employee. Following this approach often will result in a more realistic plan as well. In many cases, the employee will be more familiar with the details of his or her job, and have a more realistic perception of what the job requires. Listen closely to the employee's suggestions and, where appropriate, build them into the plan.

STEP SIX
ENSURE EMPLOYEE UNDERSTANDING

> *Ensure that the employee understands. If there are any questions, make sure you clear them up at this point.*

Finally, ensure that the employee understands the performance elements and standards that have been established. In other words, make sure that he understands what it is that you expect him to do in order to obtain fully successful ratings on each performance element. If there are any questions or apparent confusion, make sure you clear it up at this point.

It may be necessary to have two or more meetings to accomplish these objectives, particularly if there are substantive changes that need to be made as a result of the first meeting. It is also a good idea to have the employee sign the overall performance plan to acknowledge an understanding of the its contents. This step will make your job easier since it acknowledges the employee's understanding and ensures, in most cases, that the employee will accept the plan and work toward meeting the standards that have been set.

If the employee refuses to sign the plan for any reason, it is a good idea for you to note on the plan the date that it was explained to the employee and that she declined to sign it.

Following these steps will lead to more efficient performance. If your employees understand the organization's goals, objectives, and priorities, it will be easier for them to work more effectively and to improve the performance level of the entire organization. The time you take to analyze and explain these goals and objectives in relation to individual positions through development of sound performance appraisal plans will be a great help in this process.

Evaluating The Employee

The first time an employee formally receives feedback from you on progress under the performance appraisal plan will be during a progress review. Remember, a *progress review* is:

> **A review of an employee's progress in meeting established performance standards at various points during the performance period.**

Performance regulations require that you conduct at least one formal progress review with each employee during the appraisal period. Some agency plans require more than one progress review at regular intervals during the appraisal year. Meeting with an employee more frequently to review progress is usually a good idea anyway, regardless of whether additional meetings are required.

Therefore, even though a progress review is planned during the appraisal period, do not feel you have to wait until a regularly scheduled, formal review to meet with an employee to discuss work performance. Routine, frequent progress reviews often result in a variety of benefits both for the supervisor and for the employee, including far fewer surprises and hard feelings at performance appraisal time. Here are some of the benefits you can expect.

Better Communication

An employee may be hesitant to discuss problems with you or other supervisors for a variety of reasons. A progress review will help you determine whether any problems exist in meeting the job elements and performance standards. The progress review may also provide an effective way to confirm that an employee truly understands the standards and elements.

Coaching And Counselling

During a progress review, you will have an opportunity to determine whether the employee needs advice or other assistance in meeting the requirements of the performance plan. By arranging a formal meeting, you will have a chance to encourage the employee to express any problems encountered during the appraisal period and to ask for any assistance necessary. If additional training or closer supervision appears to be necessary based on your discussion, you will know about it and be able to take necessary corrective steps long before the end of the appraisal year.

More Feedback

The progress review allows you to give employees detailed feedback on how well they are matching up to the established performance standards during the appraisal period. Remember, the purpose of the appraisal system is not to surprise the employee at the end of the appraisal cycle, but to help him (and your organization) meet its performance goals throughout the year. If you have a problem with an employee's performance, the employee should know that and be reminded of your expectations during the review. This is also a good opportunity to point out the things employees are doing well, and to boost their enthusiasm and confidence.

Modifications To The Performance Plan

If work requirements have changed since you developed the performance plan, or if you see other good reasons that it would be a good idea to modify the elements or standards in it, a progress review is a good time to make the needed changes. You should make necessary changes to the plan in the same manner as you put together the original plan. That is, you should write the performance elements and standards using the same techniques discussed earlier, and discuss them and the reasons for the changes with the employee thoroughly.

Employees sometimes suggest modifying performance standards during the appraisal year. For example, an employee may suggest changes to the plan because of changes in workload, changes in workplace technology or methods, or changes in her control over some elements in the plan.

You should consider such suggestions carefully, and give the employee a direct answer and your reasons for it.

Note that you should avoid making changes to performance standards that are not absolutely necessary if they are to take place near the end of the performance appraisal year. Last minute changes could affect your ability to render a performance appraisal on the established schedule if the employee is left with less than the required time to work under the new standards before being rated.

Again, it is a good idea to have the employee sign the amended performance plan to signify that he received it and was provided an opportunity to discuss the changes with you.

THE PERFORMANCE RATING

The purpose of the final performance appraisal discussion is to let the employee know where she stands and to issue a performance rating based on her performance during the entire appraisal cycle. The appraisal that you issue becomes a formal record that is maintained by you and the personnel office. It will be used in making decisions on a variety of personnel actions.

PREPARING FOR APPRAISAL MEETINGS

There are several steps you can take to obtain the maximum benefit from the performance appraisal discussion. First, prepare for it. If you have not thoroughly reviewed the employee's plan and the employee's actual work accomplishments, the appraisal discussion will be superficial and not very useful either for you or the employee.

Know what points you wish to make prior to the appraisal meeting and know why you want to make those points. The best way to do this is to carefully review both the performance standards and all data and recollections you have that provide useful examples of the employee's actual work performance. Be ready to discuss how your observations translate into the specific rating you have selected for each element in the performance plan.

REVIEW EMPLOYEE INPUT

In many instances you may have obtained the employee's views on his performance during the appraisal period before issuing your rating. This is particularly true in situations in which you are not completely familiar with the employee's work because of the large number of people under your supervision or because of the technical nature of the employee's work. Depending upon the employee's position, you may also want to discuss his performance with clients of your organization.

This will enable you to obtain a more complete picture of an individual's performance before rating each element in the performance plan. Increasingly, organizations are experimenting with different ways to gather input from the employee's co-workers as another important data point for appraising performance. (See Chapter Five's discussion of team performance and 360 degree feedback as an example).

Explain Your Rating On Each Element

Third, provide the employee with a thorough explanation of his or her performance on each of the elements in the performance plan. Wherever possible use hard data and actual examples to illustrate and explain how you reached your conclusions as to the proper rating for each element. It is important to keep the discussion professional and objective, however. Avoid being drawn into arguments or recriminations. If things start heating up, take steps to cool them off, even re-scheduling or postponing part of the appraisal if necessary.

Praise Good Performance

Fourth, praise good performance. Nothing is worse than an evaluation that focuses solely on performance deficiencies and negative comments. Most employees' performance is good overall, with room for improvement in a number of areas. Make sure to spend time on the employee's successful accomplishments as well as those areas in which he could do better. Any person likes personal praise. When justified, it encourages most employees to continue doing a good job and to strive to do better.

Concentrate On Performance

Avoid being drawn into discussion of things that are not really directly involved in an employee's performance, such as conduct problems or personality traits. Concentrate on the actual work performance you have reviewed or observed. Remember, the purpose of the performance review is to review performance — not the person.

Don't Sugarcoat It

If there are negative aspects of an employee's performance, do not skip over them to focus on more pleasant topics. You must discuss the negative as well as the positive aspects of an employee's performance even though it is often unpleasant to do so. Failing to discuss negative concerns is unfair to the employee, and ultimately to the public. Remember that the employee must have an opportunity to improve. If there is a performance problem, she is entitled to your opinion even if one of you feels uncomfortable discussing it. Unfortunately, failing to point out such problems usually ensures the problems will continue. It also denies your agency the benefit of the improved performance you should be encouraging and requiring.

Encourage the Employee

Finally, encourage each employee as much as possible to accomplish performance objectives. Every employee has good traits and these should be emphasized at the end of the session, even if it has been necessary to spend some time on performance shortcomings. A rule of thumb that many supervisors find helpful is the sandwich approach to performance appraisal meetings. That is sandwich the bad news between the good news. To do so, open the meeting on a positive note by focusing on an area of positive accomplishment, then address performance problems, but end on a high, encouraging note by closing with review of further positive comments.

Remember, you can also use this opportunity to identify and discuss possible improvement strategies — such as training or developmental assignments — that could be used to strengthen performance where needed.

Avoid Common Pitfalls

There are several common problems that happen in performance appraisals that you should avoid.

1. Giving all employees the same rating.
Those who have done a good job should be recognized and rewarded. Those who have not done a good job should receive help in improving their performance. Giving all employees the same rating will reward mediocre or substandard performance, and discourage greater efforts by other employees. It is easier to yield to the temptation to rate everyone in the middle in the short run because it avoids controversy. But in the final analysis, your organization will be harmed by it.

2. Rotating higher ratings to make everyone happy.
Ratings of outstanding or highly successful should not be rotated just to keep everyone happy. If an employee truly deserves a rating above the successful level, telling the employee to "wait for his turn" will not motivate a good performer — it only allows the supervisor to avoid taking the responsibility for doing the job that needs to be done.

3. Applying the "halo effect".
A halo effect is letting recent events or one event that occurred during the rating period affect the total appraisal. Remember to rate the employee for the entire appraisal period, not just on one assignment or only the most recent events.

4. Confusing performance with personality or conduct.
Remember that you are appraising a person's performance, not her personality. Consciously avoid treating those employees you personally like better than those you may dislike based on your emotional responses to them. By separating performance from personality and focusing on standards and actual work performance, you can keep things on an objective and fair level — and avoid charges of favoritism and unfair rating.

Taking Action Based On Performance

After you have issued the final performance rating, it may be appropriate to take a personnel action based on the rating. The action you may wish to take, if any, will vary widely depending upon the circumstances. The options available to you include the following:

> *The action you may wish to take, if any, will vary widely depending upon the circumstances.*

Quality Step Increase
If an employee is under the general schedule (GS) pay system, she may be rewarded with an additional step increase after receiving an outstanding performance rating, or the highest rating your organization permits. This action results in a base pay increase and it is cumulative in that future pay raises (such as cost-of-living raises) are based on the higher pay level.

Within-Grade Increase
An employee who meets the time-in-grade requirements and has received a rating of fully successful or higher is eligible to receive a within-grade increase. A within-grade increase boosts the employee's base pay rate.

Performance Award
As a supervisor, you may wish to recommend an employee for one of a variety of performance awards based upon the rating you have given or special accomplishments the employee reached during the rating period. Such awards do not raise an employee's base pay but may include a lump sum cash payment.

Promotion
Performance ratings may serve as a factor used to decide whether to promote an employee to the next grade on a career ladder.

Completion of Probationary Period
A performance rating may be used to determine whether an employee should successfully complete the probationary period. Following completion of the probationary period, the employee is entitled to more substantive procedural rights in an adverse action.

Reassignment

Based on performance, a decision may be made to place an employee in a different position. In some cases this is done to allow the organization to benefit from a particular skill evidenced during a rating period that could be better used elsewhere. In other cases, a reassignment may be used as an opportunity to perform successfully in another position because he has not performed successfully in the present one.

Training

As a supervisor, you may want to nominate an employee for training opportunities. This may be done to enhance proficiency in an area where a person has demonstrated noteworthy capability. It may also be used as an attempt to bring an employee's skill level up to a higher standard.

Demotion or Removal

If an employee is performing at an unacceptable level on one or more critical elements, demotion or removal may be an appropriate action. Note that when taking such an action, the employee must first have been given an opportunity to demonstrate acceptable performance after assistance has been offered during an established *performance improvement period*.

Reduction in Force

An employee's performance rating can become extremely important during a reduction in force. Federal law assigns years of service credits for the last three ratings of record if they are fully successful or higher. This can significantly affect how the employee fares in a RIF.

In taking any of these actions, consult with your personnel advisor to ensure the results of your efforts are proper and timely.

How OPM's 1995 Regulations Change Performance Standards

The Office of Personnel Management (OPM) revised its performance management regulations in the Fall of 1995. The regulations give agencies more flexibility in setting up a performance management system. While most aspects of performance standards continue unchanged, there are a few noteworthy items you should know about.

Team Performance Standards

Agencies can now develop team performance standards for organizations where teamwork is the key to successful organizational performance. Therefore, if the work of the team is generally more important to your organization than the work of individual employees, you may wish to develop team-based performance standards that evaluate the contributions of the team as a whole.

> *You may wish to develop team-based performance standards that evaluate the contributions of the team.*

Some readers may be thinking something like this: "If I write all standards as team performance standards, I can give those standards to employees all at once. And, at the end of the appraisal period, I can call everyone in at once, tell them they have done a good job, inform them that I'll see them at the same time and place next year to talk about performance appraisal, and send them back to work."

Good strategy, but it's not that simple. Why? Because OPM has placed in its regulations a requirement that each employee's performance plan include at least *one individual critical element.*

The law still requires that everyone receives an individual appraisal. So you're still going to have to deal with employees individually when setting standards and giving appraisals. The new regulations, however, provide a more logical method for recognizing teamwork than our current performance appraisal system.

ADDITIONAL PERFORMANCE ELEMENTS

The regulations provide for a new category of performance elements called "additional performance elements."

> *Additional performance elements may not be used in deriving a summary level rating.*

Additional performance elements differ from critical and non-critical elements in that they may not be used in deriving a summary level rating (such as "outstanding" or "fully successful"). On the other hand, they may be used for other purposes, such as making award determinations.

How can agencies effectively use additional performance standards? Here's an example: Let's say an agency did a great deal of its work in teams, and it wanted to acknowledge the work of these teams. By adding an "additional element" such as "contributions of the team towards organizational effectiveness," the agency could assess and reward the contribution of the team without making that element part of anyone's individual performance plan.

On the other hand, if the agency wanted to assess the individual's effectiveness as a team member, the agency could develop a "team behaviors" critical or non-critical element, and measure this as part of an individual performance plan. You can also remove an employee for unsatisfactory team behaviors if the element is considered a critical one.

As you can see, adding these additional elements can add a flexibility to the performance management process.

Pass/Fail Standards and Appraisals

The regulations allow you to use as few as two levels for assessing performance on elements and for summary ratings, *if your agency adopts a two-level approach to performance appraisal.* That means you could be using terms such as "pass/fail," "in/out," or "successful/unsuccessful" when assessing the performance of employees.

> *This change would also provide you with a different way of looking at employee performance.*

This change also provides a different way of looking at employee performance. With only two levels, you'll basically be asking yourself what standard of performance determines whether an employee is retained on the job. Looking at things that way may actually make it easier to write performance standards. You won't have to worry about "highly successful" or "minimally successful performance" in a two-level system.

But with this approach, you will still need a way to acknowledge the work of those superstars, the "pass +" employees. Unless your work is solely done by teams, you'll probably need some way of determining how to reward remarkable individual performance. This may require you to write a memo to higher management or perhaps rank your best performers through a forced distribution process. The regulations will allow you to do that.

360 Degree Appraisals

While 360 degree appraisals are more closely related to performance measurement than performance standards, it's still an important point to mention.

> *This process gives access to a much greater depth of information about the employee.*

A 360 degree appraisal system allows you to use information obtained from a variety of sources in determining an employee's rating. In addition to supervisory input, data may be provided by co-workers, peers, subordinates, customers, vendors, and others. The data is obtained from a wide variety of sources (hence the title "360 degree" appraisals). While the supervisor continues to provide the overall performance evaluation, this process gives her access to a much greater depth of information about the employee.

While this aspect of performance appraisal is still in its infancy, agencies using this approach give it high marks on both validity and reliability. And it allows the supervisor to obtain information from people who may have closer daily contact with the employee.

SUMMARY

Used properly, an effective performance management system will result in a better managed organization and higher employee morale. You should be sure to work closely with your personnel office as you implement a sound performance management system.

ABOUT THE AUTHORS

Ralph R. Smith is President of FPMI Communications, Inc. He has worked in a variety of personnel and labor relations positions for federal agencies including the U.S. Customs Service, Department of Education, Office of Personnel Management, Department of Labor, Federal Labor Relations Authority and the National Aeronautics and Space Administration. He has authored a number of articles and books on the federal human resources system.

Dennis K. Reischl is a partner and founder of FPMI Communications, Inc. Prior to this, he advised and represented management at the General Services Administration, Office of Personnel Management, Department of the Navy and the Wisconsin Electric Power Company. He has authored a number of articles and books on the federal human resources system.

Smith and Reischl also edit four newsletters for federal employees: *The Federal Labor & Employee Relations Update, The Federal Manager's Edge, The MSPB Alert!*, and *The Federal EEO Update*.

Gary Koca is Associate Director of FPMI Communications. He joined the company after a successful 26-year career in human resources management with the Chicago Region of the Office of Personnel Management. For approximately ten of those years, he was OPM's Chicago region "expert" on performance management. Gary has taught many courses and written many articles on various aspects of the federal personnel system.

FPMI PUBLICATIONS

- Career Transition: A Guide for Federal Employees in a Time of Turmoil — $10.95
- Performance Management: Performance Standards and You — $ 9.95
- Dealing With Organizational Change — $ 6.95
- EEO Today: A Guide To Understanding the EEO Process — $ 9.95
- Managing Effectively In A Reinvented Government — $ 9.95
- Managing The Civilian Workforce (2nd Edition) — $ 9.95
- The Bargaining Book (3rd Edition) — $12.95
- The Supervisor's Guide to Drug Testing (2nd Edition) — $ 9.95
- Federal Manager's Guide to Total Quality Management — $ 9.95
- The Federal Manager's Guide to Liability — $ 9.95
- Effective Writing for Feds — $ 9.95
- Practical Ethics for the Federal Employee (2nd Edition) — $ 9.95
- Sexual Harassment and the Federal Employee (2nd Edition) — $ 6.95
- The Federal Manager's Guide to Preventing Sexual Harassment (2nd Ed.) — $ 9.95
- The Federal Manager's Guide to EEO (2nd Edition) — $ 9.95
- The Federal Employee's Guide to EEO — $ 6.95
- Federal Manager's Guide to Leave and Attendance (3rd Edition) — $ 9.95
- Federal Manager's Guide to Discipline (2nd Edition) — $ 9.95
- The Ways of Wills — $14.95
- The Federal Manager's Handbook — $21.95
- Improving Employee Performance — $ 9.95
- Supervisor's Guide to Federal Labor Relations (3rd Edition) — $ 9.95
- Welcome to the Federal Government — $ 6.95
- Using Alternative Dispute Resolution in the Federal Government — $ 9.95
- A Practical Guide to Using ADR in the Federal Service — $ 9.95
- RIF's and Furloughs: A Complete Guide to Rights and Procedures (2nd Ed.) — $14.95
- Working Together: A Practical Guide to Partnerships — $ 9.95
- A Practical Guide to Interst Based Bargaining — $ 9.95
- Empowerment: A Practical Guide for Success — $ 9.95
- Team Building: An Exercise in Leadership — $ 9.95
- Managing Anger: Methods for a Happier and Healthier Life — $ 9.95
- Dynamics of Diversity — $ 9.95
- Voices of Diversity (hardback) — $22.95

PRACTITIONER PUBLICATIONS
- The Desktop Guide to Unfair Labor Practices — $25.00
- The Federal Employee's Law Practitioners Handbook — $59.95
- The Federal Practitioner's Guide to Negotiability — $25.00
- The Union Representative's Guide to Federal Labor Relations (2nd Ed.) — $ 9.95
- Permissive Bargaining and Congressional Intent: A Special Report — $19.95

Shipping: 1-10 Books: $4; 11-50 Books: $12;
51+ Books: Actual UPS Shipping Rates

PRICES EFFECTIVE THROUGH
DECEMBER 31, 1996.

FPMI NEWSLETTERS

The Federal Labor & Employee Relations Update
Subscription Fees   12 Months $225

The MSPB *Alert!*
Subscription Fees   12 Months $125
L&ER Update Subscribers pay only $95

The Federal EEO Update
Subscription Fees   1-9 Subscriptions $175 each

The Federal Manager's Edge
Subscription Fees

1-50 Subscriptions	$65 each
51-100 Subscriptions	$59 each
101-500 Subscriptions	$52 each
501-999 Subscriptions	$45 each
1000+ Subscriptions	$39 each

PRICES EFFECTIVE THROUGH DECEMBER 31, 1996.

ELECTRONIC NEWSLETTERS

The Electronic Edge

Subscription Fees:
1. One year subscription $200. This price includes one 3 1/2" floppy disk, one paper copy and the right to reproduce an unlimited number of copies to distribute throughout one organizational location.

2. Two year subscription: $375

3. Three year subscription: $510

The Electronic Federal Labor & Employee Relations Update

Subscription Fees
1. One subscription $595. This price includes one 3 1/2" disk, one paper copy and the right to reproduce an unlimited number of copies to distribute throughout one organizational location.

2. Two year subscription: $1,095

3. Three year subscription: $1,510

The Electronic EEO Update

Subscription Fees
1. One year subscription $595.00. This price includes one 3 1/2" disk, one paper copy and the right to reproduce an unlimited number of copies to distribute throughout one organizational location.

2. Two year subscription: $1,095

3. Three year subscription: $1,510

FPMI Video Training Packages

VIDEO TRAINING PACKAGES

• **Managing Cultural Diversity**
Package includes 25 guidebooks with workshops; a facilitators handbook with suggested workshop answers and a script with techniques to conduct a training session on cultural diversity; master copies of vu-graphs; and a 28 minute video on implementing cultural diversity in your agency. ($695 for the complete set.)

• **Dealing With Misconduct**
Package includes video program, 25 guidebooks and 25 copies of *Federal Manager's Guide to Discipline*. ($695)

• **Writing Effective Performance Standards**
Package includes video program, 25 guidebooks and 25 copies of *Performance Management: Performance Standards & You*. ($695)

• **Managing Under a Labor Agreement**
• **Managing Under the Labor Relations Law**
Order separate courses for $495 each. Special package includes both video programs with 25 workbooks for each course and 25 copies of *The Supervisor's Guide to Federal Labor Relations*. ($895)

• **Sexual Harassment: Not Government Approved**
• **Preventing Sexual Harassment: Some Practical Answers**
Order separate courses for $495 each. Or purchase our special package of both video programs with 25 workbooks and a leader's guide, 25 copies of *The Federal Supervisor's Guide to Preventing Sexual Harassment* and *Sexual Harassment and the Federal Employee*. ($895)

Additional workbooks for each class are also available.

Quantity discounts are also available on all tape purchases.
Call for more information. (205) 539-1850.

FPMI TRAINING PACKAGES

TRAINING PACKAGES

• **Resolving Labor Management Relations Issues Through Partnership**
Includes 25 copies of the Participant's Workbook, one copy of the Instructor's Guide, 25 copies of *The Supervisor's Guide to Federal Labor Relations* and *The Union Representative's Guide to Federal Labor Relations*, plus master copies of overhead transparencies. ($595)

• **Practical Ethics Training for Government Managers and Employees**
Includes 35 copies of the Participant's Workbook, 35 copies of *Practical Ethics for The Federal Employee*, one copy of the Instructor's Guide, and master copies of more than 50 black & white overhead transparencies. ($595) Color transparencies and color slides available at additional cost.

• **Effective Equal Employment Opportunity Leadership**
Includes 25 copies of the Participant's Workbook, 25 copies of *The Federal Employee's Guide to EEO*, 25 copies of *The Federal Manager's Guide to EEO*, one copy of the Instructor's Guide, master copies of more than 50 black & white overhead transparencies. ($595) Color transparencies and color slides available at additional cost.

Please call for more information on these packages.
Quantity discounts available.
(205) 539-1850 or fax (205) 539-0911.

FPMI SEMINARS

FPMI Communications, Inc. specializes in training seminars for Federal managers and supervisors. These seminars can be conducted at your worksite at a flat rate that is substantially less than open enrollment seminars.

The instructors for FPMI seminars have all had practical experience with the Federal Government and know problems Federal supervisors and employees face and how to deal effectively with those problems.

Some of the seminar-workshops available include:
- Building Productive Labor-Management Partnerships
- How To Use ADR and IBB
- Interest-Based Problem Solving
- Negotiating Labor Agreements Using Interest-Based Bargaining
- Negotiating Labor Agreements (Traditional)
- Pre-Retirement Seminar
- Taking Adverse and Performance-Based Actions
- Labor Relations for Supervisors
- Preventing Workplace Violence
- Resolving Organizational Conflict
- Managing the Dynamics of Organizational Change
- Making Discipline & Performance Decisions
- Managing Problem Employees Effectively
- RIF
- Developing Effective Performance Standards
- Developing Team-Based Performance Standards
- How to Review Performance with Employees
- Performance Management: New Rules, New Opportunities
- Working Together in a Diverse Workforce
- Preventing Sexual Harassment
- Effective Personnel Management for Supervisors & Managers
- How to Interview People Without Getting Fired, Demoted or Successfully Sued
- Effective Government Leadership in a Downsizing Environment
- How to Build an Effective Team in Your Agency
- Change Leadership for the '90's
- Handling ULP Disputes Effectively
- Preparing and Presenting Your Arbitration Case
- Practical Ethics and The Federal Employee
- Basic Labor Relations for Practitioners
- MSPB Advocacy
- Effective Legal Writing for Personnelists & EEO Officials
- Administrative Investigations and Report Writing
- Women in Management
- Time Management

For more information contact:
FPMI Communications, Inc.
707 Fiber Street
Huntsville, AL 35801-5833
PHONE (205) 539-1850
FAX (205) 539-0911
Email: fpmi@aol.com
Internet: http://www.fpmi.com